A Widow's Journey...
Healing a Broken Heart
For those who are grieving the loss of the love of
their life...

Believe in your eternal love connection...

Believe in your eternal love connection...

Believe in your eternal love connection...

I dedicate this book to my dear husband Eddie it is a tribute to our eternal love in life and in death.
May our awakened spirits always be one.
Love is the only thing that truly exists.
I love you Eddie with all my heart,
I will always love you...

Believe in your eternal love connection…

Table of Contents

Chapter

Introduction

Introduction

I cannot begin to explain the unbearable grief that I felt after my husband's death. This unbearable grief came from the depths of my soul, it came in waves, it overwhelmed me, and it drained my spirit. In the beginning I fought hard to control it but it was uncontrollable. I fought hard to ignore it but it remained steadfast and uppermost in my thoughts both day and night. I was in deep despair. I was in the darkest and loneliest days of my life. All my life I had been strong and now I felt weak and vulnerable.

For months I lost my way, my bearings, and my direction in life. My identity had changed. I felt that I was walking alone in life. I knew God was by my side and Eddie was in my heart but it was hard to be alive. I kept telling Eddie that this was the hardest thing that I have ever had to do in my whole entire life. I told him I loved him, and that I needed him. I told him that a part of me died with him, and I didn't know how I would go on without him.

When I thought of myself I saw a huge hole in my chest where my heart should have been. I saw myself curl up into a small ball and drift off into space. That's what I wanted to do curl up and drift away. I tried desperately to control my grief but I was unable to, it controlled me. It would creep into my thoughts. I felt my loss from the moment I awoke until the moment I fell asleep. My only comfort came from my daughter who was also suffering this unbearable grief as well. She was close to her father and she loved him so very much. To this day she is the only one that understands. She was protective and concerned, she promised Eddie she would take care of me, she shared my grief, and her love for me is what kept me alive...

Grief has its physical signs as well. In my case I felt sick to my stomach. Even now when I think of our walk through the valley of the shadow of death I feel sick to my stomach. I'm not sure when or if this will end. When I think of his hospital stay I feel his pain and his anguish. I try not to think of it because it hurts too much.

As I look back, I realize how difficult the first two years after my husband's death were. In fact they have become a blur, a time in my life where nothing mattered, a period of the greatest sadness that I have ever known. I want you to know that this sadness is something that never completely leaves you. This great sadness remains with you hidden deep inside. As time passes you just learn to accept it. You accept the sadness in your heart, and you learn to cope. Our society doesn't like to talk about death and dying, our society believes that all you need is time to heal, when in fact you soon realize that this great sadness will remain with you until you are reunited with the one that you love so very much. I have learned to cherish this sadness as a part of our undying love for each other…time passes but our love remains…

When you have been married for as long as we were (35 years) it is extremely difficult to think of yourself as just "you;" for so many years we were "us". In the years that Eddie and I were married I guess you would say that we really weren't very social people. Oh, when we were young we had lots of friends but as we grew older we were happy just to be "us". We shared the same passions and being "us" was all that we needed. I have thought about meeting new people but for now I am content…I am still happy just to be "us"…

Although I know that according to our Earthly rules I am now a widow, which means I am now just "me"; when in fact in my heart I am still "us".

So, secretly I decided not to accept being just "me." I decided I wasn't going to accept society's new identity for me. Secretly I decided not to accept the title of widow. I chose to secretly rebel against certain societal rules of widowhood. I still wear my wedding ring proudly. I still use Mrs. Paula M. Ezop on any correspondence. I left my husband's name on our checking account. Yes, I realize that some people would say that I am in denial. But the truth is I really don't care what people think. What I do know is that even though society has given me a new identity. Even though society chooses to call me a widow, I do not think of myself in this way because I am still connected to him through our love. And, so I secretly carry out my rebellion against widowhood and all of the silly rules connected with it…

As I said before the first two years of my walk alone have become a blur. I thought at the time that my thinking was rational, and now I realize that it may not have been. Instead, when I look back I see that it was a time of gaining strength and perspective. It was a time when grief overwhelmed me, and I struggled to find my life again – our life again. Each day was a struggle of utter sadness and despair. But, I found my way. I found my way strengthened by his love. I like to believe that someday we will live in a world that will recognize and understand the spiritual connection that can be made and maintained beyond the veil. Someday mankind will realize and accept that Heaven and Earth exist together, and that our loved ones spirits still remain very much a part of our lives.

I needed to find a way to bring happiness back into my life. For me, it is as if my life has now gone full circle. I find myself finding joy and happiness in doing things that we first did together when we were young. My passions for decorating and gardening have been reignited. My energy has returned, and my writing has found new direction. My writing is my new identity – not widowhood but being a writer is my new identity. I guess what I am trying to say is that you need to find your passion and that you will find your passion. You need to find what will bring joy and hope back into your life if you are to survive. Find your passion and you will find your new identity. Find your passion and you will find your direction in life.

In my heart I know that Eddie will always be with me. He hears my thoughts and he still shares my life with me. Oh, I know that he isn't here physically with me. No, he is with me spiritually - connected through our love. So, I feel that we do have a future together. I feel that this is what we were meant to do. We were meant to stay connected through our love. Maybe that is what we were here to learn in this lifetime.

I know that you know what I am talking about. You hear them in your mind. You speak to them with your mind. Thoughts come into your head when you need their help. There have been many instances where I have known for sure that he has helped me. Usually it is when I am trying to fix something around the house. I can hear him telling me which tools to use or how to go about fixing something. The same thing with the car, I can hear him tell me that it is time to get the oil changed and the tires rotated. He is still with me… Oh, I know that a lot of people would say that this is all in my head but I know that it isn't. I believe so strongly in their existence, and even though it can't be proved I know that they remain with us guiding us and helping us when we are in need. As I continue to walk alone I wonder what the future will hold.

I know that Eddie is still in my life but he is in the Heavenly world and I am in my physical body here on Earth. Could I ever remarry? Would anyone ever be able to take his place? These are all questions that go through my mind at times. In the thirty-five years that we were married we never discussed what the other person would do if one of us would die. The question of whether they would remarry was never a part of our conversations. My heart and intuition tell me that there will never be another man in my life. I am happy to stay connected through our love, and I look forward to the future with great anticipation of further spiritual growth and understanding of life beyond the veil.

The death of my husband tore apart my world. This book contains my innermost thoughts as I came to grips with his death. My writing helped me deal with my terrible loss. Chapters in this book were written at various times as I grieved. There is one recurring theme, and that is that we remain connected through our love. I call it the love connection. This love connection is what enabled me to survive after the death of my husband. As you read my words it is my hope that you too will be able to focus on your love connection as you struggle with your loss...

My Story

I am now sixty-eight years of age. Nine years have passed since the death of my husband. I can't believe it has been nine years. Some days it feels like yesterday, and other days it feels like forever. Each year as Spring approaches I begin to feel the approaching doom. You see my husband passed away on April 26, 2005 and the signs of Spring trigger the memory of those horrible days before his death. I don't think I will ever again look at the coming of Spring with happy anticipation. This is my story. It is a love story that now reaches beyond the veil.

I know that there are so many others whose stories are the same as mine. There are people who have lost their husbands, their wives, their sons and daughters, their brothers and sisters, and their friends. There are people who have been touched by the deaths of people they don't even know, yet they share in the tragedy of their deaths through their heartfelt love and compassion. The story that I tell is our universal story of undying love. These pages lay bare the heartfelt love that we all have for those we loved so deeply. Those who we loved and lost.

Believe in your eternal love connection…

I never thought for one moment that I would be without the love of my life, not at age fifty-nine. No not me, it could never happen to me. Even now, after all this time there are times that I mutter to myself in the early morning hours that I can't believe it. This wasn't supposed to be my life. You see, the possibility of my husband's death never even entered my mind. In my heart we were still the young bride and groom that entered that beautiful neighborhood church on our wedding day. We were so young and so in love. I still picture us standing in front of the candle-lit altar. The church was filled with the fragrance of flowers, we were young, and on the top of the world.

We had waited for this moment since the evening Eddie asked me to marry him and I said, "Yes." What a magnificent and endearing memory. I can still hear him repeating our marriage vows, he was so emotional, tears filled his eyes as he pledged his love to me. It was a hot, rainy, summer day, August 9th, 1969 to be exact. Yes, if I close my eyes I can still see and feel the church. I can feel the love that we shared that day. Yes, if I close my eyes we are back in front of the altar saying, "I do." It was a day bursting with love. A wonderful day filled with joy, and a day of great beginnings. Eddie and I were beginning our lives together. We vowed to love each other in sickness and in health, for richer or for poorer, until death do us part.

"Until death do us part," now when I hear those words I smile and I think that those vows are all wrong because I still love my husband beyond death. I still love him. He is and will always be my husband throughout eternity. "Until death due us part," sounds final. This finality is an ending that even now I cannot bring my heart to accept.

Our marriage was a new beginning, and I feel that his death is also a new beginning not just for him but for "us." His death and new existence are a new beginning in "our" lives. I continue my spiritual journey here on Earth, and he continues his spiritual journey in Heaven. Believe me it has taken years of healing to allow me to look at his death in this way. Still even though I know this to be true there are days when my heart feels the pain all over again. There are days when grief washes over me and I lose all sense of reason. There are days that I cry out to heaven in loneliness and despair. But, those days are much fewer now. Is it acceptance of his death? Or is it the spiritual love connection that we have made? I believe that it is the spiritual love connection that we have made that allows me to accept my new existence.

It is our love that has connected us beyond the veil. It is this great love connection that makes my life bearable without him physically here on Earth.

We never thought about life ending. We never contemplated life apart. No, we never considered being without each other. In fact, I thought that we had forever together, or at least until we were eighty or ninety years of age. Now, when I look back I think how presumptuous of me. How naïve it was of us to presume that we had forever to be together. Common sense tells you that we all are going to die some day. That's it, some day – not today, not tomorrow, not on Sunday, or Monday, but some day we are all going to die. Was it presumptuous of me or was I somehow remembering another existence? Did I know that we do have an eternity together?

Yes, in my heart I felt that we had forever or at least until some day came into our lives, and that wouldn't happen for a very long time. Oh, how wrong I was. Eddie, my husband of thirty-five years (almost 36) passed away on April 26th, 2005. He was sixty years old. We were high school sweethearts, lovers, and best friends. He was my life and my heart's inspiration. A day doesn't go by that I don't think of him often. I still feel his love and he is still present in my life. We did everything together and we are doing this together. We are surviving together even though he is in a different world than I am. We are connecting through our love. Even though I can't see him I feel his presence and I know that he still exists. I know that he would never leave me because he loved me too much to ever leave me. In my heart I now know that we do indeed have forever. Not forever in our physical bodies but forever as spirits who are a part of the light, and surrounded by God's love.

When Eddie died I searched for a book that would help me deal with my loss. I wanted a book that would explain his existence. I wanted someone to tell me that he was all right. I needed to know more about the mystery of death and his new spiritual existence. I was lost without him. My heart was broken and I had lost my way. I never found a single book that would help me deal with his death in the way that I wanted to deal with his death. What I did find were books that explained the different stages of grief that I would go through. I found books that told me in time I would be able to move on. But, that isn't what I wanted to hear. How could I say good-bye to the man I had walked through life and death with? No, I wouldn't move on without him, I wanted to stay connected in some spiritual way, and I wanted to know that it was possible.

The world of spirit opened its doors to me during the darkest days of my life. I spoke to God throughout my husband's illness, through his death, and after his death when my grief consumed me. God was there when I needed him, he was there when my lost my bearings, and he was there when I questioned his wisdom. He never left my side.

Sharing my journey with you is not easy for me. But, this is something that I feel I must do. And, in my heart I know that you will benefit by hearing my words. I pray that my words will comfort you, and open your hearts to the love connection that exists for us all.

Believe in your eternal love connection…

Our Love Story

I want you to know, "us" (Eddie and me). I want you to know our love story. I want you to know that we were just ordinary people living an ordinary life, and how our lives changed overnight. I want to tell you about the love that we shared and continue to share. I'd like to take you back in time to when my husband and I first met. We both attended high school in the city of Chicago. It was the 60's. We were young and carefree. Although we lived blocks apart we had never met. Fate does have a way of entering your life. My best girlfriend in the whole world was dating Eddie's best friend. One evening they decided (unknown to either of us) that we should meet, and they arranged a blind date. Well, neither one of us knew that we were going on a date. We thought that we were going to a high school play with our friends. We didn't know that someone else would be there. Well, that is how I met the love of my life, on a blind date arranged by our two best friends.

Eddie was a half-year ahead of me and he graduated 6 months before I did. At that time the Vietnam War was in full swing. Two months after Eddie graduated he was drafted. Luck was on his side and he spent his Army career at Fort Bliss, Texas. He never had to go to Vietnam. I was in college back then, we corresponded and we spent his leaves together. Now as I look back I realize that we never grasped the danger of the situation. We never thought that death would enter our lives then, even though there was a war going on. When you are young you never think of the possibility of death. No we never grasped the danger of the situation, after all we were young and in love.

Eddie asked me to marry him, and of course my answer was, "yes!" We had a beautiful August wedding and we couldn't have been happier.

I taught second grade and Eddie was in the printing trade. Two years later we bought our first home (a real fixer-upper). We were living the so called "American Dream." Our daughter was born and we were happy!

Life went on, and soon we bought a new house in the suburbs. We did the usual things, parties, graduations, and vacations. You know the usual things that ordinary middle class people do. When you are young you think that you will live forever. We felt that way into our 50's. That is until the death of our parents. It was their deaths that gave us an awareness of our mortality. But, you put that in the back of your mind. We were still young at heart and we had our health. How things change.

Our lives up until then had been normal. Both of us were blessed with good health... I thought. My husband was hospitalized for three weeks. He was in and out of intensive care, and transferred from hospital to hospital. He spent his last days in the cancer ward of one hospital, under hospice care. In this ward they were all too familiar with dying. Again, I prayed, we prayed, we promised, we asked for a miracle and my daughter and I never left his side. We were with him when he died and I still picture him as he took his final breath. That overwhelming sadness has never left my heart. I will always feel that gut wrenching pain as he was taken from us.

God said, "No" to our prayers for a miracle. Was it God's will? Was my husband's spirit ready to return to him? Do we as individuals make our own life and death decisions despite what others are praying for? These were all questions that I asked myself.

It's strange how people react to you after the death of a spouse. They feel uncomfortable. They ignore you and the subject. They see the pain in your eyes, and they feel your loss even if they won't talk about it. You do need to talk about it. I wanted our lives back again. I wanted those long Sunday afternoons together, the family dinners, the laughter and the tears. I wanted "us." Everyone says that time heals. No, time leads to acceptance, and if acceptance is a form of healing then yes time heals. You learn to accept and to live with your loss. But, it is a loss, a terrible heart breaking loss that never goes away. The grief and sorrow have a way of sneaking up on you when you least anticipate it. Tears will stream down your face as the waves of sorrow come from the depths of your soul and overwhelm you. They overwhelm you with a force so strong that you feel the pain that you felt when you saw him take his last breath. Yes, that terrible moment frozen in time, when you saw the love of your life, the man you shared your heart and soul with depart from you in that one brief fleeting moment of time as your world stood still. Your world now changed forever, and ever, and ever. Oh, how you long to be with him.

Throughout our lives my husband and I confronted life together, and we always knew there were answers. Even in death I knew there was an answer. I would not say good-bye to him. I knew deep in my heart that his spirit was alive and well, and if he could be with me even after his earthly body was gone he would be.

Believe in your eternal love connection…

My life as I knew it was gone. The love of my life, my reason for living, my heart's inspiration was gone. I wanted to curl up in a ball and drift off into space. I felt that like a wounded animal, and I wanted to crawl off somewhere and die. I found it hard to be around people who knew us. I suffered in silence as I went about the tasks of living. I know in my heart (as I have mentioned before) that this is the hardest thing that I have ever had to do. Yes, the hardest thing I have ever had to do is to continue on by myself without my partner's physical presence.

As I heal or accept his death, I am beginning to understand the transformation from death to living in the light. You see our thinking is all wrong. Spiritual life is forever and our physical existence is but a brief moment in time, a brief moment in our eternal existence. Survival, strengthening of our spirit, and growing the light and love of God is all that is important. Although, even though I believe that this is true my spirit still dwells in my physical body, and the wound in my heart runs deep.

I think back to the hurried mornings of days past when my husband was alive and I realize now how we took those mornings for granted. I remember watching him shave, the sounds of his dresser drawer closing as he took out his socks and shirt for the day, and the sound of the garage door going up as he left for work. Our minds were filled with thoughts of the day, of work, of traffic, and of what we were going to have for dinner. We both went about our hurried morning and the house was filled with the sounds of our morning routine. Now, the house is eerily quiet except for me. Those mornings are now cherished memories known only to me, so many memories that I hold close to my heart. I pray to God that these memories will never fade because these are the things that keep him close to me.

It has been nine years since my husband died and still as I get ready for work my thoughts are only of him. I just can't get used to my aloneness, I just can't get used to my walk alone. In my mind it is still "us." After thirty-five years of marriage I can't begin to think of myself without thinking of him. There are some days where I still feel him so very close to me.

I find myself telling him out loud that I know that he is here, and that my wish at that moment is that I could see him. I pray to God to let me see him. But, all that I can do is to see him so very clearly in my mind's eye. He is no longer sick, in fact he looks like he did when he was young. Oh he was so strong and so very handsome. For a brief moment it is almost as if nothing has changed and then in an instant I am back to reality.

The house that I lived in after my husband's death was the house that we lived in together for 30 years, and everywhere I turned there was a memory. It was a large house for one person, three bedrooms, 3 bathrooms, a basement containing his workshop, and a yard filled with memories of barbeques, Fourth of July celebrations, and cool October nights together. This was the house that our daughter grew up in. This was the house that we enjoyed together. This was our home. This was "us." It became a place that at times was so very hard for me to be in and yet a place that I couldn't be without.

I spent my weekends taking care of that house – our house. I found that my husband taught me well – he tackled any and all jobs around our house with vigor and determination. When those jobs were left to me, faucets that needed to be fixed, loose boards on the fence to be nailed down, a furnace filter to be replaced, all the weekend projects of owning a home – I took on those jobs with the same vigor and determination that he did for this was the house that he loved and was so very proud of. This was our house, and somehow those projects brought us close together once again. I could hear his voice telling me what tool to use, and what drawer of his workbench it was in. And, for a brief moment we were "us." I stayed in that house for five years. It took me that long to leave. I now live in a townhouse close to my daughter. I have been able to put that existence behind me, but it wasn't an easy decision to make. It was a decision that I had to make to move on. I could no longer live in the past...

Believe in your eternal love connection…

Reminders of my Aloneness

After Eddie's death, there were constant reminders of my aloneness. The harsh reality confronted me countless times a day in the smallest of ways, mundane things that previously I wouldn't have given a second thought to became large psychological challenges in my day – as I walked alone. For instance, who would think that coming home from work, making dinner, and sitting down to eat at the kitchen table would be cause for a meltdown? I couldn't bring myself to come home from work, make dinner, and sit down to eat at the kitchen table, it was just too sad to have a meal at the kitchen table without him. He loved to cook and he would always cook dinner for me. Sitting there alone would just be a cruel reminder of his absence. Also, who would think that cooking in the kitchen you cooked in for 30 years would cause emotional pain beyond comprehension? I avoided cooking for months. The kitchen was my husband's domain. He was everywhere in our kitchen from his handwritten recipes to his favorite pan or spoon. Gradually, I overcame the sadness of cooking in his kitchen. It was probably out of necessity. However, I ate downstairs in the family room as I watched television. Eating there with the sound of the television became my routine, and although I was still alone I was not reminded of the past. The most difficult part of my aloneness was being alone in the bed that I shared with the love of my life, the bed that we shared for 35 years. It was here that the harsh realities of my aloneness tore open the deep wound in my heart. I still sleep on my side of the bed…there are just some things that I just can't change and in my mind that is how it should be. In a way I guess I'm keeping him alive in my world through small insignificant things that have now taken on significance for me as I face my aloneness... together yet apart…

I found myself reacting in the strangest of ways to the silliest of things. One such thing was the grocery store. For the longest time I couldn't bring myself to go grocery shopping at our newly built grocery store. You see my husband always did the grocery shopping, and yes, he spoiled me. Before he passed away they were building this new grocery store, and he was really looking forward to shopping in the new store. After he passed away and the store was completed I refused to shop there for about a year. Even though this store was closer and had lower prices I just couldn't bring myself to shop there. Like I said the silliest of things. Now, I think that in a way I was protesting not only the store but also I think it was my way of protesting the fact that he died. It was as if he couldn't shop in the new store then I wouldn't either. I finally reached a point where I told myself that I had to get over it, and that I needed to confront whatever was holding me back from going into that store, and I did. It was just one of those silly things that I just couldn't do as I learned to walk alone.

Even though I have accepted his death I still feel in my heart that it is still "us". I cannot bring myself to get rid of all of his clothes, they belong to the "us" part of my life and I just can't do it. If I do it will no longer be "us" in "our" house. So, for now some of his clothes are in the closet or in the dresser drawers. When and if the time comes that I feel I can continue my life without his clothes I will. But for now his dresser remains full, his jackets are still in the closet, and his cap remains in the back seat of my car, and we are still "us".

This aloneness thing often over powers me. No matter how hard I try to be strong, awful realizations hit me and my confidence dwindles to that of a young woman, and suddenly I am no longer the independent confident woman that I had become.

I find myself thinking about all the "what ifs." What if I cut myself really bad – who is going to help me? What if I fall down the stairs and break a leg - who will help me? What if my car won't start – who will help me? What if I lock myself out of the house? What if I get stuck in the snow? There is no end to the awful scenarios that my mind conjures up. I have learned that I can't let the "what ifs" occupy my thoughts and control my life.

I walk alone, something I never thought I would be doing. This walk alone becomes sheer torture on the days of celebration, the holidays, the birthdays, and the anniversaries that we shared together as "us." Even writing about it brings tears to my eyes for these are the days when my heart cries out and the pain is almost unbearable. These are the days when walking alone is all too real. I've tried making new traditions to help me get through the saddest of days, but I will be honest with you I haven't been very successful. The cherished memories together on these special days just cannot be replaced. As hard as I try to stay positive it is on these days, sadness and grief rear their ugly heads with a vengeance, and I plummet down into that vast abyss of sadness as waves of grief wash over me.

Believe in your eternal love connection…

As I try to get comfortable in my walk alone I have this terrifying fear in my mind that I will forget him. Yes, there is a fear that I will forget him, forget his voice, forget "us". But how could I ever forget the love of my life? It is only a fear, a fear that I know I will overcome in time because I know in my heart that I can never forget the man that I loved with all my heart and soul, the man who was and continues to be my heart's inspiration.

You see, in the end my walk alone comes down to my finding ways to accept and endure the loss without forgetting. I work at finding ways to cope with the simple everyday things, and continue to remember. You see I need to find ways to still be "us" in a physical world that sadly is now just "me." There is no magic potion to take. I can only persevere, and hold tight to the belief that our love will continue to keep "us" connected – you see our love is the magic that I seek as I continue to walk alone.

Others Don't Really Understand

In my mind, the only one who truly understands what you are going through is another widow or widower. I think back to how I treated my mother when my father died, and I can see how insensitive I was to her. I think about the words I said to her and how inadequate they were. I could not understand her sudden outburst of tears. I had no idea of the pain that she was feeling. I didn't understand how alone she must have felt. I just didn't understand. I had lost my father, and I felt a terrible sadness, but not the horrible heartbreak that she must have felt.

You see, unless you have lost the love of your life you have no idea of what it is like. People may think that they do. They may sympathize with you, but when it comes down to it they have no idea of what it is like. They don't know your heartache, they don't know your fears, and they can't possibly understand your loss. This is something that you and you alone are left to deal with.

I remember speaking to my husband's aunts at his wake. They too were widows, and I wanted some words of encouragement. I wanted them to tell me when the pain would stop. I wanted them to tell me that I would make it, that I would be all right. However, they were silent. Their looks said it all. They were not all right, and they couldn't tell me when the pain and sorrow would end because they themselves didn't know. The truth of the matter was that they couldn't give me any words of encouragement because they were still struggling with their loss. I know that now, but I didn't know it at that time.

You find too that people feel extremely awkward around you when you meet them for the first time after your loss. They have a hard time looking you in the eye. They don't know what to say. They don't know if they should bring the subject up. There is an awful silence in the air – because they don't really understand, and they have no idea of how to handle this awkward situation.

It's almost like you have some terrible disease that they want to ignore. Perhaps it is best because in the beginning it is so very difficult to talk about without crying. People feel uncomfortable if you cry. Crying is a release for you but crying in public is too heart wrenching for others. Therefore, maybe it is better that they just say the niceties, and move on to another subject. After that first time, they feel more relaxed around you. They said the niceties, and now they feel that their relationship with you will go back to normal.

Believe in your eternal love connection…

They don't understand how hard it is for you just doing the everyday things like going to work, eating dinner by yourself, or grocery shopping for one. No, they just do not understand.

Perhaps the best place to go for understanding is a support group for widows and widowers. I never did this. It was my choice to grieve alone. I just didn't think I'd feel comfortable around strangers at a time like this. I guess it is an individual choice, and I can see where it would have helped. Because, another widow or widower would understand what you are going through when no one else really does.

I turned to my daughter who knew how hard it was for me. She saw me go from a self-confident woman to a woman who now was unable to make any decisions without getting another opinion. She saw me retreat inside the home that my husband and I shared for most of our life together. A place that was hard to be in, and yet a place that I couldn't leave. It was my time capsule of our lives together. She saw me lose interest in everything. She saw the joy leave my world when my husband died. She watched over me as I struggled with my new existence. Did she understand? She understood as much as any daughter could. Did she understand the depth of my pain? I don't think she could. I think only another

widow can understand the depth of the pain that we feel when our

husband, the love of our lives dies.

So, knowing that, knowing that no one can truly understand

unless they have gone through it makes it easier to understand how

people react to you. It makes it easier to understand the

awkwardness, the lack of eye contact, and the lack of understanding.

When being a widow comes up in a conversation I find

myself saying, "You have no idea what it is really like…no

idea…you can't even begin to imagine…" And, that says it all,

unless someone has experienced this terrible loss they cannot

possibly understand, and they can't have any idea of what it is really

like…they just can't understand…

Believe in your eternal love connection…

The Hurt That Won't Go Away

When you lose the love of your life there is a soul felt hurt that just won't go away, at least that is what I have experienced. Now, when I look back I guess one would expect to feel that terrible pain in their heart when their husband or wife dies. I know that it is only normal to feel that way. But, what I didn't anticipate or know was that the pain would never go away. That soul felt pain that hurt that you feel within your heart is with me every day. Yes, the heartfelt pain differs in intensity, but nonetheless it is there lingering in the background of my being.

In the first months after my husband died the pain, the hurt would turn into sadness. In the beginning, the sadness was extremely hard to deal with. In the beginning the pain, the emptiness, the terrible sadness turned into unrelenting sobs, tears, sleepless nights, and depression. I had continuing thoughts of wanting to die so that I could be with him. Perhaps then the pain would end, and happiness would enter my world again. I knew that these thoughts were selfish thoughts. I had a daughter that needed me, and I could hear my husband saying, "No, don't even think like that. We will be together again, but not yet, not now. You're time on Earth isn't over," and life would go on. I know that I will struggle with the pain that is forever in my heart.

As time went on the unrelenting sobs, tears, sleepless nights, and depression slowly went away. They would return occasionally and unexpectedly, but they were easier to control. Even to this day, I never know when I will burst into tears or become depressed. But, those moments are fewer in comparison to the first few years of my loss. Yes, the hurt is still there, it will never go away. How could it? It is a loss that I will forever carry within my heart. What keeps me going is knowing that love is eternal, and the pain that I feel, the pain that tugs at my heartstrings every day is a reminder of that eternal love.

That hurt has become a beautiful reminder of our "love connection." That hurt is our "togetherness" though we are physically apart. Yes, it has taken me time to accept my "aloneness." Time leads to acceptance, and the hurt that never goes away now oddly comforts me. We are told that we are here on earth to experience and learn from our experiences. We are told that we must look at life's experiences and ask ourselves what we were meant to learn from that experience. Truly, death and loss are one of the greatest of life's experiences. What have I learned from that horrible, life shattering experience?

I have learned that love is all that truly exists. I have learned that love is all that counts. I have learned how lucky I was to have known love. I have learned that love is eternal. I have learned that we are still connected even after death. I have learned that there is love beyond the veil. I have learned that even though we are physically apart that we are spiritually connected forever, and ever, and ever.

The hurt that will not go away is natural. The hurt that won't go away is to be expected. I wanted it to go away. I wanted my life back. I wanted "our" happiness back again. I know now that spiritual, soul felt healing does take place – that healing is a "knowing" that our love is alive and strong. Yes, that healing is an "understanding" of the love connection that we have after death.

Healing doesn't take the hurt away. The hurt may never go away. Does it have to? How could it? My healing or acceptance has taken place. You see, the hurt that I feel is now a sweet, beautiful, gorgeous, lovely, reminder of our love. I find myself smiling as I write. Looking at my heartfelt hurt in that way makes my outlook on life a little more sparkly, a little more magical… Looking at my heartfelt hurt in that way strengthens our love beyond the veil, and oddly gives me a sense of peaceful calm within my being as if I just discovered a wonderful secret of life and death. A sparkly bit of wisdom has appeared. Yes, I have received one of those cherished ahh moments. A wonderful spiritual lesson was given in the midst of darkness. Yes, the universal light of love appeared just when I needed it.

So, you see I am a widow, and I am a survivor. Am I walking alone? Are you walking alone? Alternatively, do the loves of our lives stay with us throughout eternity? I can say from the bottom of my heart that we do not truly walk alone. I can say without a doubt that the loves of our lives are with us always.

The hurt that won't go away has been transformed into a beautiful reminder of our continued love, and I am able to go on. Take that hurt that will not go away and turn it into a beautiful reminder of your continued love. You too will smile, know, trust, and believe in their existence and in their continued love for you – a love that will never end...

The Little Things That Hurt

After the death of my husband, there were so many little things that hurt me deeply, little things that brought me to tears and made life impossible. These things rendered me helpless and unable to move on, things that froze me on the spot, things that I just couldn't let go of because letting go would mean that he was truly gone, and I just couldn't accept that on an emotional level. I knew he was gone, I was there when he took his last breath, and I was there when the man I loved more than life itself left me - a moment I will never forget. Oh, where to begin? There were so many things that a normal person wouldn't even consider a reason for a melt-down. Simple things like his tooth brush in the medicine cabinet, the sound of the garage door going up, his coat hanging in the closet, his cap on the seat of the car, his handwritten note about the last time he replaced the furnace filter, the pictures of our life together, his handwritten recipes, his pillow, his workshop, the snow thrower, everything that was his or part of his life was a reminder that he was gone, and these things broke my heart over and over and over again. But they were things that I wasn't ready to let go of – not yet.

Believe in your eternal love connection…

It was not only things that hurt it was seeing other couples, and it was as if they were all over, holding hands, talking softly to each other, laughing together, grocery shopping together, doing all the things we used to do together. It hurt me to see them so happy, oh how I missed him. I missed his smile and even his frown, I missed his touch, I missed his embrace, and I missed us! I missed him next to me in bed. I refused to sleep on his side of the bed instead I tried to remember how it was when he was laying next to me. I thought of his snoring, and his getting up in the middle of the night when he was unable to sleep. Oh how I missed him.

Now, time has passed and the little things that hurt so badly are fond sweet memories of the life and love that we shared. I have left his cap on the backseat of the car where it belongs, a memory that he is still with me no matter what. His toothbrush is still in the medicine cabinet but it no longer hurts to look at it. The leather jacket that he loved still hangs in the closet, you see there are some things that I just can't part with, and that's alright. I am glad that I have these things, sweet reminders of him that make my life bearable and that have helped me. The little things that hurt so badly have become a beautiful remembrance of him.

Believe in your eternal love connection…

It still hurts to see other couples together but not as much as it did that first few years without Eddie. I want you to know that the little things that hurt so badly will turn into beautiful memories that you will hold close to your heart. The hurt goes away and in its place is a beautiful memory of your life together.

Memories are what will help you. I can still remember his touch, his embrace, his smile, his frown, his mannerisms, everything about him – even his scent when we first danced together at a high school dance so many years ago. Yes, he is alive and well in my memories as it should be. I know that you are afraid that you will forget them. I was afraid of that too, I was afraid that I would forget his voice, forget his touch, forget the love that we shared, but I haven't. How could I forget? I'll never forget, and that puts joy in my heart and it is what carries me through the sad days. Yes, I still have sad days, days when I miss him so much, days when I cry myself to sleep, but those days are fewer now, and the little things that hurt so much are now the things that keep him alive in my heart...

I've been thinking a lot about the writing of this book lately, wondering why it has taken me so long to write this. I can't help but think that there is a reason. I can't help but think that there is a reason that I am writing this nine years after my husband's death. I hear spirit whispering that there is a reason, and I know what that reason is. In my heart I feel the reason is that I needed to turn that corner in my journey, I needed to see how things turned out before I wrote the book. I needed to know how our love grows even beyond death, and I needed to tell everyone about their "love connection." I needed to speak of how it was when I first lost him, and how it is now that so much time has passed. I needed to go further on my journey to be able to help others.

I know in my heart that you will be helped by my experience as you try and heal from a terrible heart wrenching loss. The little things do hurt, the little things can render you helpless, but in the end it is the little things that will become a remembrance that will carry you through the darkness and into the light and love of life once again... with the one you loved with all your heart right beside you...

The Horrible Dreadful Holidays

For so many years, I have struggled with the holidays. The struggle begins the moment a holiday approaches, no matter what the holiday is Christmas, New Year, Easter, Memorial Day, Mother's Day, Father's Day, or the Fourth of July. Each holiday carries with it a precious memory of our lives together, and the holiday accentuates that feeling of loss and aloneness. So, yes, no matter what the holiday I consider it a horrible and dreadful day, and I'm not going to sit here and tell you that those days will get better, nor am I going to tell you about some magical way to get through them. Because, the reality is that there is no magical way to get through the holidays without feeling that emptiness and heartache.

Believe me I've tried every conceivable way to make them better, and I haven't found a solution to the depression that consumes me when a holiday comes around. That first year after my husband died when a holiday would roll around, we would try celebrating it just like we used to. Everyone put on a good front, but the family was miserable without him, and the spot where he always sat at the dinner table was a reminder of his absence. Then, there was the year that I decided we needed to start some new family traditions. Instead of eating at home we'd go out to a nice restaurant maybe that would be better. That wasn't the answer either, we just missed him, and it didn't matter where we were because he wasn't there. If it were up to me I would just try to ignore the holidays but then there are the children, and you want them to remember the holidays and the family traditions.

This year I am doing my best to just muddle through, I'm telling myself that the day will pass and I'll feel better. The terrible loneliness that I feel, the pain in my heart will be gone until the next holiday arrives and the cycle will continue. So, this is the year of muddling through…

Each holiday I pray to God to take the sadness away, some holidays I'm able to dismiss the pain until the actual day arrives, and yet other holidays I feel the dread for an entire month leading up to the holiday. I guess that as widows and widowers we just have to accept this as a way of life – the horrible dreadful holidays. We accept it and try to hide our pain from our families, crying ourselves to sleep at night, keeping our thoughts to ourselves, and remembering the wonderful years that we celebrated the holidays with the love of our life. Yes, remembering and holding them close to our hearts as we do every day.

As I write spirit is telling me that I've forgotten the most important thing, the only thing that really matters. In my mind's eye I see in bold capital letters, "**LOVE**". Love is the only thing that matters, and on these tough emotionally charged days, we have to remember that we are still and always will be connected by our love. The love that we share is eternal, and one day we will be together again. The magic that we seek to get us through the holidays is our love. Our love will take away the heartache and pain. Our love will connect us, and enable us to bring joy back into our lives if we let it.

Know, accept, remember, and cherish the love connection you have with your spouse, this is what will make the holidays bearable, this is what will keep you out of the darkness of despair and in the light of eternal love!

Spirit works in amazing ways. I began this part of the book not knowing what I could possible say about getting through the holidays. In fact, I had been feeling down because Easter was approaching. So, on Good Friday I decided I just had to get away for a night. Maybe that would help me handle the approaching holiday. Not only was it the holiday but the anniversary of his death was only a few days away… So, I booked a one night stay at a resort that my husband and I loved to go to. (I've felt that I should come up here for about a month now, something was telling me to come here. I've always felt a spiritual connection here because of the solitude, and because Eddie and I loved it here.) Last night I just relaxed, and I thought I would write for a while in the morning before I left. I looked at my outline and "The Horrible Dreadful Holidays" popped out at me, and I began writing.

My heart ached because I would be alone on yet another holiday. But as I wrote, I found the answer that would help to ease my heartache. The way to get through not only the holidays but life itself is to stay connected through our love. Stay focused on what matters, know, trust, and believe that love is eternal. That is the magic that we seek, and that is the reason I was told to come here on this weekend – to find the magic that we need, and to try to continue to heal my broken heart.

Once again, I am amazed at how spirit works in our lives. What makes this revelation even more amazing is that the last time I was here I was given the titles of the chapters to this book. Once again I had felt that I needed to come here, I thought that there was a book to be written but I didn't know what. I felt that spirit would reveal what that book would be. Well, I was here all weekend, and nothing happened. Then, in the morning just as I was getting ready to leave, chapter upon chapter came to me. I could hardly write them down quick enough. Yes, amazing how spirit works!

Miraculously as I write spirit is helping me to heal, helping me to find answers not only for myself but for all of us. This is truly a miraculous journey of love… And, this revelation has taken one of those horrible dreadful holidays, and turned it into a magical, miraculous, and amazing journey… Even more thought provoking is that the holiday is Easter…a spiritually charged time in the lives of so many of us…

The Wounded Spirit

No one can quite understand the terrible, gut wrenching pain, that a woman feels when she loses the love of her life. No one that is, but another widow or widower. As I look back I realize how spiritually connected we had become. I was married to my husband for thirty-five years, and as I have often said, "We were high school sweethearts, we were lovers, and we were best friends." But, I never really realized that our spirits had become one – we were spiritually connected, and our souls were united as one. It was another one of those "Ahhh" moments. No wonder I felt so alone, no wonder I felt lost, no wonder I felt, "wounded," my spirit had been tragically separated from the man I loved completely.

Yes, "wounded" is the perfect word to describe how you – your spirit feels when you lose the love of your life. I pictured this big hole, this "wound" in my heart, and it hurt terribly. I wanted to roll up into a ball and drift off into space. My walk even mimicked how I felt. I found myself sort of shuffling my feet, my head down, and my smile gone. I felt old. I constantly fought back tears that were always just below the surface. I felt sick to my stomach. I felt out of control for the first time in my life. This was something even

I couldn't fix. This was something that I hadn't planned on, and there was nothing anyone could do or say to make it go away. In my mind, the only thing that could take away the hurt that could heal the deep "wound" in my heart would be if Eddie (my husband) would miraculously come back to me. I pictured him walking in the door as if nothing happened. I saw him lying in bed next to me. I saw him sitting in our family room, and watching our favorite movie together like we did so many times. I knew it wasn't possible but that didn't stop me from imagining that it could happen.

People aren't aware of the wound in your heart. They expect you to be sad for a few weeks, or maybe a few months and then just snap back into being yourself – "moving on," as they say. But how can you move on after such a terrible loss? I couldn't. I lived in a house that said "us." I lived in a neighborhood that was "ours." I had few close friends because our life was "us." We enjoyed just being "us." So, when you suddenly go from "us" to just "you," how can you move on? How can you say good-bye to the life that you shared? I couldn't. Could you?

Then there are those old sayings that everyone says because they don't know what else to say. You know things like, "It just takes time," or "In time you'll be able to move on," or "Time heals all wounds." I've found that time just brings acceptance. The wound is still there. After nine years when I visualize my heart I don't see the gaping hole, instead I see scar tissue where the hole once was. Have I accepted his death? Or, have I found a new way to exist with him beyond the veil? I believe that it is a little bit of both. I no longer believe that he will walk through the door one day as if nothing ever happened. And, I have found a new way to exist with him beyond the veil. This has helped to heal my broken, wounded heart.

As married couples we focus upon the physical world. Our lives revolve around the physical, the house, the kids, the vacations, the holidays, and the list goes on and on. Our days are filled with all of these things. Our concerns are for the physical life that we lead. What we don't consider is the spiritual connection that we have, and rightly so. There is no need, no awareness of the spiritual connection because we don't have to. Our world is the physical world.

However, when you are married a transformation takes place between your spirits. Unknowingly, you become one in spirit. That is why when one spirit leaves the physical plane, and travels to the spiritual realm, the pain and anguish is so unbearable. Your united spirits have separated and it hurts. The good news is that this spiritual separation is temporary. You can if you want to, stay spiritually connected. (I didn't realize this until much later.) Had I been more spiritually aware when my husband passed away perhaps the pain wouldn't have been so bad? I don't know. What I do know is that his death has brought me a spiritual awareness that I never knew existed.

When my husband died, I cried out to God. I told him that he had this all wrong. I told him that I couldn't go on without him. I told him that maybe, just maybe I could handle this if I knew he was all right, if I could only talk to him – maybe, just maybe I could handle this. I cried like I never cried before, it was guttural, almost like a wounded animal. I couldn't stop it. I rocked back and forth wishing that I too were dead. I had thoughts of dying in a car crash and joining him. Or, maybe I would just fall asleep and not wake up. Horrible thoughts that I couldn't shake, that was until I decided that I would find a way to know that he was all right. I was determined that I would find a way to communicate with him. I was going to survive by staying spiritually connected – that was how I was going to fix this!

Amazingly, I am able to picture him in my mind's eye, and we do talk. We have made that spiritual connection beyond the veil, and I have survived the darkest days of my life. I want you to know this so that you too can survive the darkest days of your life.

I'm not a psychic. I've never had any special gift. I'm just like you are. I loved my husband just like you loved your husband or wife, and I decided that if others can speak to those who have passed on to the spiritual realm then so can I. That's all. I just made up my mind that it wasn't good-bye. I made up my mind that I was going to stay connected to the love of my life in the only way that I could. I had to find a way to heal my broken heart, and staying spiritually connected was my way of healing my broken heart.

I read as many books as I could on the subject. I learned to meditate. I learned how to make contact beyond the veil – you see I had to try. Psychic readings, spiritual connections are no longer the taboo subject that it once was. Today, it is widely accepted by many. Some say that there is a thinning of the veil. There is certainly a greater understanding of the subject.

Today, my wounded spirit has healed, and I have accepted his death. I have survived the darkest days of my life with the help of my husband. I believe in his existence, and I know in my heart that we are still connected, and will one day be united once again. Until then, I am going to stay spiritually connected in the only way possible.

Know that they are all right and that they are very much involved in your everyday life. Know, trust, and believe that you are still one in spirit, and that the love of your life is still with you. Believe me coming to this realization will help you immensely. You will heal your wounded spirit. The gut wrenching pain and anguish will diminish, the tears will subside, and laughter will return to your life, as you remain one in spirit…

The Darkest Days of My Life

Brought the Spirit World into My Life

I have always been a spiritual person, but after the death of my husband my spirituality seemed to suddenly blossom, and fill my life in amazing ways. I found spirit opening up to me. Serendipitously on a regular basis, I would find books and articles to read. I read everything I could get my hands on about death and dying. Then, as I grieved I found myself being directed to read books about after death communications. I just had to learn more about communication with those we loved who had passed on. I just couldn't let go of the love of my life. Physically he was gone but our love lingered on. In fact it got stronger each day – I could feel it, spirit-to-spirit, and heart to heart I could feel his love, and it was healthy and strong.

I can truly say without a doubt that you can stay connected to the one you love. Although, we can't see, taste, or touch love we know it exists. This energy, this invisible force, is the love that we hold in our hearts that keeps us forever connected. It is the "love connection." The beautiful thing is that we all possess this love connection. You have the ability to stay connected to those you love, to those that have transformed from the physical world to the spiritual world by using your love connection.

When my husband died I told God that he had this all wrong. I told him that I thought that I could handle the physical walk alone if I could just talk to my husband. I needed that communication to survive the darkest days of my life here on Earth. I had to know that Eddie was all right. I had to know that we were still "us." I needed to stay connected to the man I loved. God did not disappoint me, He heard me, and my husband and I have used our love connection to stay in touch even though he is in the heavenly realm, and I am here in the physical world.

In the beginning I thought that it must be my imagination when I would hear my husband talking to me. I know now that it never was my imagination. Spirit was leading me, guiding me on a miraculous journey. Showing me how to use that love connection to communicate – it was just that simple. We all have a sixth sense and the love connection is part of that sixth sense. You see, you too can stay connected to the man or woman that you love if that is what your heart desires – just let spirit into your life, and follow your heart…

Believe in your eternal love connection...

Believe me I know how painful it is to be a widow or widower. Believe me I know how difficult each day can be for you. Believe me I know how difficult the holidays are. Believe me I know the heartache. Believe me I know the sadness and unexplainable tears that appear out of nowhere. Believe me I know...I am a widow...

Know that spirit is at work in your life. Open your heart and mind to see and hear the sparkly spiritual miracles and guidance that are given to you each day. Believe me when I tell you that opening your heart to spirit makes the widow's or widower's walk a walk of spiritual healing. It becomes a journey that heals the terrible pain of loss. Your own personal spiritual healing journey will be one of unbelievable discovery. It will open up an entirely new world of communication and support that you never even knew existed.

This is written for you. I'm just an ordinary woman who faced what you are facing. I hope that the spiritual lessons that I have learned will help you...

I know deep in my heart that you will find joy in life once again. Just remember, love never dies, love never ends, and death is but a new beginning. Believe in your love connection...

Believe in your eternal love connection…

Finding Your Way Out of the Darkness

When the love of your life dies you become immersed in darkness, it surrounds you, it consumes you, and it is with you day and night. This darkness is your new reality, a reality not of your choosing. It is a horrible gut wrenching existence that drains you and controls you. You are cloaked in a veil of emotional darkness like you have never felt before, and there is no magical way to rid yourself of this horrible feeling. Every minute of every day, you live with this empty feeling. This is what having a broken heart feels like. You feel empty – a part of your heart is missing – the love of your life is gone, your world is turned upside down, and there you are in this lonely abyss, this vast empty wasteland, which is now your life. It wasn't supposed to be this way, you had plans, this just couldn't have happened to you – but the reality is that it did. How do you deal with this darkness? How do you carry on when your heart is broken? How do you find your way out of the darkness of loss?

Sadly, you and you alone are the one who has to face this new reality. It is up to you to find your way out of the darkness. There is no timeline, and the darkness does not adhere to any rules. No holds barred – the darkness can rear its ugly head at any time and in any place. You are on an emotional roller coaster going through a long tunnel of pain and despair – that's the reality of your new existence. I know I've been there. But there is an end to this roller coaster ride. You will find your way out of the darkness of despair and into the healing light and love that surrounds us all.

Your life has been changed forever, but if you are like I was, you struggle to try and keep your former life intact. You try to keep things as they were, but of course you can't because that way of life is gone forever. You soon find that out, and struggle with this new dark and lonely existence.

So, how do you find your way out of the darkness? How do you rid yourself of this empty feeling? How do find your way into the sunlight? When my husband first died the darkness consumed me. I cried, and cried, and cried some more. I cried out to God, and told him how much it hurt. I told him that this was the hardest thing that I ever had to do, and I cried some more. The darkness still has a way of sneaking up on me from time to time, and I cry some more. Tears were a release for me and still are. They helped me to find my way out of the darkness.

I cried until there were no more tears. I've cried myself to sleep, and felt better in the morning. Crying helps, it seems that after a good cry things seem a little better. Tears are an emotional release in your battle against the darkness of grief. Tears are a way of healing the pain that you feel. Even now there are days where I can't control the tears. I don't always know what triggers the tears, but the sadness still finds its way into my heart. (I think that this sadness will always be a part of our lives.) Now, I ask the angels to take the sadness away, I ask them to help me and they do, amazingly after a little while I feel much better.

Another thing that helps you to find your way out of the emotional darkness is to keep busy. My husband and I were always working on projects around the house. So, when he passed away I dove into painting, cleaning, and maintaining our home. I felt so close to him when I did these things, I felt as if he was watching me, and even telling me how to do something (especially when I tackled the electrical and plumbing projects). As I write this I can see him smiling, shaking his head in agreement, and saying, "You scared the hell out of me when you worked with the electricity." I probably did scare him because when I think back I really didn't know what I was doing. So, find something to throw yourself into, whether it is around your home, with a church group, school group, or neighborhood organization. Find something that you are comfortable with and something that you enjoy. Believe me, it helps, you might not feel comfortable doing any of these things right away, but you'll know when you're ready.

My daughter and I spent hours and hours talking about all of the good times, talking about my husband and how much we loved him. This was a tremendous help to me. I think it was the biggest thing that helped me find my way out of the darkness. Talking about him kept him alive in our hearts and in our minds, and it still does to this day. We speak of him often, and when we do we can feel his love surround us. Love never dies, and the memories are a gateway to that love. So, never forget, always remember and your loved one's love will surround you and enfold you with a warmth that you can feel so very strongly.

Finding your way out of the darkness is a slow and gradual process. As I mentioned, there is no timeline. No one can tell you how long you will feel this darkness because everyone's journey is different. What I can tell you is that it does get easier. You will reach a point where you conquer the darkness, where you can control it, where it no longer controls you. You will reach a point where you realize that it is possible to live in this new existence, and allow joy to once again enter your life. One day you will wake up and know that things are going to be alright.

It's not an easy journey, but you will find your way. You will rid yourself of that horrible empty feeling, and it will be replaced with a knowing. One day you will know deep in your heart that your loved one still exists, and that you are still connected through your love – your love connection. Yes, one day you will feel this love connection, and you will know that your love will never die, and that one day you will be reunited again. The darkness will no longer have a hold over you, where there was darkness there will be love and light. A love and light like you've never experienced before...

Staying Centered

When you are filled with grief it is important to stay centered, to find a place within where you can put everything in perspective, a place where you can still feel their love, otherwise that tremendous sense of loss will completely consume you. I had to keep myself centered in a good place, in a place where I felt our love, and where I knew that everything was going to be all right. I had to stay centered for the majority of my day, in order to live my new existence, and to survive and heal.

We all have moments of despair, but they can't be with you all day long, they just can't. You need to survive and know that your loved one wouldn't want you to grieve forever. You have to find your strength and bring yourself out of the darkness of despair, and into the light of love. Once you know in your heart that the love you have for each other survives even death, you will be able to grow stronger and stronger every day. You will be able to find that place within where you feel their love, you will find the center of your being, and you will be able to know, trust, and believe that things will get better.

Believe in your eternal love connection...

Knowing that the love that you had still exists between you even after death is what will help you to stay centered. That love that you cherished will create a good place in your heart and in your mind. I know, I have been there, and believe me without the knowledge of our eternal love my journey would have been entirely different.

Meditation will help you to connect to that love that you still share. I meditate in the morning before I get up and at night when I go to bed. The house is quiet and I am able to quiet the chatter in my mind and connect to that love. I don't know how I would have survived without connecting to that love – I really don't know...

Close your eyes and just let spirit guide you, ask your angels and guides for help in making the connection with the one you love. You will be amazed at what happens. (There are also many meditation programs available that you might want to try. We connect in different ways, you will find just the right meditation, and the results will be amazing.)

Staying centered, and connecting to the love that you still share brings you closer to each other, and it is a major guiding force on your healing journey...

The Things That Helped Me Heal

So far I've spoken about the things that hurt us so deeply after the death of a spouse, but I want you to know that there are things that help you heal. I'm not going to give you a list of things that you can do to help you heal because I don't believe such a list exists. Oh, how I wish it were that simple. Some experts talk about the stages of grief, and some experts discuss ways that you can heal. But unless someone has experienced the death of a spouse how can they possibly know? How can they feel what we feel? There are no rules, there isn't a norm, everyone is different, and grief must run its course. I am not an expert I just want to share with you what I have experienced after the loss of the love of my life.

As I confronted the agony, the horrific pain, the terrible loss that I felt so deeply I started to see that slowly, very slowly, that I was beginning to find my way. It didn't happen overnight, in fact I can't even remember when it started, but I can tell you that I began to heal or accept… At first, it was the memories that helped me along the way. It was the Valentine's Day card that I found in his top dresser drawer that made me smile, and made me feel his love surrounding me. (In fact, for many years, I would put out that card on Valentine's Day as a part of our "love connection," and it helped.) It was the high school yearbook with his note and signature to me during my junior year, and it was the cards and notes that he wrote to me when he was in the service. Little things that I came across brought him closer to me, and I felt his love, the sadness was still there, but I felt his love, and it gave me hope that I would make it out of the darkness with Eddie still by my side...

I believe you reach a point where you realize that they are not physically coming back. I know for a long time I expected him to walk through the door as if nothing had happened. In fact, I prayed that it would happen. I dreamt about it, I thought he would never leave me, he will be back I know he will be back – if anyone can come back from death it will be him. The rational side of me knew it could not happen, but the lost and alone me wanted to continue to believe that it was a possibility.

Healing is a slow process, it is an uphill battle, and for each of us the battle is different. My world as I knew it was torn apart, and the one person who I always leaned on, who I counted on was not there to deal with it with me. It was a terrible feeling of helplessness. Then I was able to see that I was the only one who could make things better. Little things built up my confidence making me feel that I could physically survive on my own. Things like making simple decisions, getting the oil changed on the car and having the tires rotated, cutting the grass on my own for the first time, using the snow thrower, and conquering cleaning the gutters. I think I needed to prove something to myself. I needed to know that there was nothing that I couldn't do if I had to. I needed to know that I could handle life.

Learning that I could get through holidays and past milestones was also something that helped to make me stronger emotionally. For years, I dreaded all holidays. While others were enjoying the upcoming celebrations, I was in denial. While others anticipated days off from work I was dreading them, knowing the emptiness and sadness that I would feel. Oh, I'd put on a happy face for my family and try, but privately I was back in the dark abyss of sadness and loss.

Then, after six years of dread, I suddenly turned a corner. I don't know why or how, all I can tell you is that suddenly I knew enough was enough. I couldn't go on like this any longer, I couldn't stand the sadness. Just one day I knew that part of grieving was over and I was going to focus on the love that I felt so strongly. In my mind, I heard Eddie cheering and saying, "Finally love!"

I know that I can make it through my birthday without a complete meltdown. I know that I can go on a long weekend by myself and have a nice time. My grieving has transitioned to a knowing, a trusting, and a believing that we are still spiritually connected and always will be. I know that spiritually he will be my rock, my anchor, just as he was in my life. I know that he will never leave me and that he will always be there for me until we meet again…

Grieving is a part of healing, it is a letting go of how things were, and learning to live with how things are. It is finding your way out of the darkness, and into the light and love that is still present in your life. The little things that helped me heal may not be the little things that help you heal. But I know in my heart that you will heal, I know in my heart that you will find your way out of the darkness of sadness, and into the light and love that you still share with your soul mate. One thing is for certain, and that is love never ends, it lasts throughout eternity, and it always surrounds you. Be open to feeling that love, and embrace the spiritual connection that exists between two worlds…it is there…it is an unseen force

stronger than life itself…

Widow and Widower's Scar

When my husband died, part of my spirit died with him. I lost all joy in life. I lost a part of my soul, and I carry a scar upon my heart – a widow's scar. Today as I write this I wonder how many wounded spirits, how many wounded souls do I pass by each day? How many widows or widowers do I walk by who appear to be enjoying life, while all the while inside they are dealing with the terrible heartbreak that they face every day and every night? How many women and men carry the widow or widower's scar upon their hearts?

I know what you are going through because I have been there. I know what you are going through because I too tried to hide the terrible sadness that was within my heart. After all, we are expected to move on. We are expected to continue our lives without the love of our lives beside us. Expectations are that after a while you will adjust to your circumstances and move on. Will your spirit ever be fully healed? How do you overcome the terrible heartache? How do you rid yourself of the scar that is upon your heart? Or were you meant to rid yourself of the scar?

Believe in your eternal love connection…

There's no easy answer on how to heal your spirit, or if it will ever be completely healed. And, no one ever talks about the scar upon your heart. I do know one thing for certain, and that is even the smallest amount of healing takes time. It takes time, and it takes a concentrated effort on your part. Even after all these years I still struggle. Even after nine years, I wake up in the middle of the night longing for my old life back again. I know it's not possible, but I still wish I could go back in time and be "us" once again. Yes, each day is a struggle to find meaning to life. But, things get better. The periods of sadness don't come as often. The laughter becomes more frequent, and slowly, ever so slowly the spirit heals. Will we ever be the person that we once were? I don't think so... I mean how could we be?

Each one of us is different. Each one of us will find joy and healing in different ways, and in different places. My writing gave me purpose and had a healing effect upon my spirit. I also took up watercolors and painted the numerous visions of angels that I had and continue to have. So, I think the bottom line is that you must find your passion. Find something that will give you purpose. Find something that will give you a reason for getting up each morning, something besides your 9 – 5 job. Maybe it is community service, or getting more involved with your church. Find something to put the joy back in your life, and slowly, ever so slowly your wounded spirit will start to heal.

I'm not sure that my spirit will ever completely be healed. I don't know when the heartache will be a thing of the past. I can't say whether I will ever be the person that I once was. But, then again, maybe that's how it is meant to be. Maybe our heartache is meant to be a reminder of the beautiful love that we share. Maybe it is meant to stay with us until we are united once again with the love of our life. Not that we are to grieve for the rest of our lives. Not that our spirits can't heal. Not that we can't find joy again. But, maybe that widow or widower's scar upon our hearts needs to be there. Maybe that scar is heaven's way of reminding us of the love that we still share with our husbands and wives. I never really thought about it that way until I started writing this book. This is the second time that I've come to that conclusion. Spirit seems to be at work here. Yes, the heartache, the scar that we carry inside our hearts is a beautiful reminder of the love that we still share…it will always be a part of us…the widow or widower's scar is a part of our love connection…

Heartfelt Thanks

Thank you for reading my book, I feel a sense of peace now, knowing that I have shared my journey with you. I know in my heart that writing this book is something that I was meant to do. However, completing this manuscript wasn't easy – I struggled at times, believing that what I had to say wasn't important. I questioned if it would be of help to anyone. As I struggled I kept hearing a soft voice telling me that I had to finish... I believe that it was spirit telling me how important it was to tell everyone about the love connection we have with those we love. You see there really is a love connection that reaches beyond death, a love connection that will be present in all of our lives if we let it in.

I also believe that you were directed to my book by the unseen forces of love that surround us – insistent that you be told about the eternal love connection that you have. I hope and pray that you will find that love connection that exists for all of us... and, that peace, joy, and love will once again fill your heart... I pray that you will see your future being filled with hope, and light, and undying love. I pray that you now know that your loved one will be a big part of your future. I pray that you are climbing out of the abyss of sorrow and grief that you are in. I pray that you feel released from your despair and anguish and that you feel connected to spirit. I pray that you realize that you are not alone, and that your spirit has awakened and that your life has new meaning! I pray that your strength has returned. I pray that you feel that even in death that your loved one is still with you, still sending you their love. I pray for your happiness as you continue your journey. Remember you are not alone your loved one is by your side…

Eddie awakened my SPIRIT, my SOUL, my very being... I hear Eddie say, "I love you. We can do this, we are one, and I love you so very much..." And I in return send all my heartfelt love to the man who's SPIRIT has become one with mine...

Believe in your eternal love connection…

Epilogue

As I look back at my 68 years of being on this Earth I wonder if I have accomplished what I came here to do. You see I'm under the belief that we all came here for a specific purpose – our life's purpose. Have I fulfilled that purpose? Am I doing what I was meant to do? What have I achieved?

My achievements are many, some average / normal achievements for a woman my age and from my generation. I received a college degree, I became a teacher, I married, and I gave birth to a beautiful daughter. I continued to do all of the normal things that occupy our lives – creating a lovely home for my family, gardening, taking the occasional vacation, going to parties, and barbeques, yes all of the normal things that occupy our lives…

But, what did I achieve that was outside of the norm? What did I do that came from my spirit, my soul that made me feel like I was doing what I was meant to do? Hmmm…I know…my writing…my spiritual writing and my children's stories that's what makes my heart sing, that's what I believe I was meant to do! I can definitely say that my writing is my greatest achievement.

Believe in your eternal love connection…

I've written many heartfelt articles, often not knowing where the thoughts and beautiful words came from. I've had books published, which was quite an achievement for me. All this happened late in life. Was it a life-long goal? No. My writing stemmed from a need to share what I had learned, my writing stemmed from my life and death experiences. My writing helped me heal after the sudden death of my husband…yes I truly believe that my spiritual writing has become my life's purpose.

There's still so much to accomplish, I am filled with words, ideas, story concepts, and inspirational thoughts…so much to share…the words and ideas are never ending…Yes, I have found my life's purpose late in life, and I couldn't be more certain that this is what I was meant to do.

I am filled with joy knowing that even if my words touch just one person that my purpose has been fulfilled. We are all connected and our achievements touch the lives of so many in ways that we can't even begin to comprehend. Isn't that thought simply amazing? Any achievement whether big or small is truly a miracle in itself, touching the lives of few or many, makes the achievement something to be proud of…and that is empowering in and of itself…

Believe in your eternal love connection…

About the Author

Paula M. Ezop is a spirituality commentary columnist. Her inspirational columns *Following the Spiritual Soul* have appeared in Oconee Today, a South Carolina Scripps Howard publication. They are currently in: Celebrating the Success of the Modern Woman, Esteem Yourself, and Open to Hope. She has contributed to such popular books as Chicken Soup for the Caregivers Soul and she has written the foreword to Whispers of Inspiration, a collection of both poetry and prose gathered from voices around the world.

Paula also co-authored a book in the Mommies Line, *Spirituality for Mommies,* and she has written *Sparkly Bits of Spiritual Wisdom,* which is a collection of her inspirational columns, and *Sparkly Bits of Spiritual Wisdom for Women.* However, closest to her heart is *A Widow's Journey – Healing a Broken Heart.*

Wiggles Press has published her children's chapter books, *The Adventures of Penelope Star and the Mystery of the Three Dragons,* and *Lee McKenzie's Summer to Remember* – both are the first in a series.

Paula holds the Bachelor of Arts, majoring in Elementary Education from Northeastern Illinois University. Her heartfelt and meaningful writing began as a means to overcome the loss of her husband. Paula has now written hundreds of articles and several books centering on life and faith. Her sustaining philosophy is that "we are more than the woman we see in our mirror."

Believe in your eternal love connection…

Paula's Other Available Books

Sparkly Bits of Spiritual Wisdom
A collection of her following the spiritual soul columns

Sparkly Bits of Spiritual Wisdom for Women
29 ½ Ways for Women to Get in Touch With Their Spirits

www.FollowingTheSpiritualSoul.com

31284942R00045

Made in the USA
San Bernardino, CA
06 March 2016